How Sweet the Blackbird Sings

Nance Cookson

How Sweet the Blackbird Sings

How Sweet the Blackbird Sings
ISBN 978 1 76041 650 8
Copyright © text Nance Cookson 2018
Cover photo: Blackbird, by Ian Schofield

First published 2018 by
Ginninderra Press
PO Box 3461 Port Adelaide 5015 Australia
www.ginninderrapress.com.au

Contents

At Least	7
The Elephants	8
The Cup	9
Four Letters	11
That's Joni Mitchell Singing in the Background	12
Robots	13
The Cup	15
Remembering	16
Plumb Roles	17
Diving	18
Onions	19
Tell Me Something That I Do Not Know	20
Rivers	21
Hamburger With the Lot	22
The Birds	23
Raindrops	24
The Palace	25
Statistics	26
Always in a Hurry	27
The Boa Constrictor	28
Upon Retirement	29
That Moon	30
Blue Wrens	31
Fantasy	32
Lizz Murphy Asks a Question	33
Once	34
If They Fluoridate the Water	35
Just How the Blackbird Sings	36

At Least

My aching feet
Won't take me
To the places
Where I'd like to roam.

But I thank the God
Who made me
That at the very least
I have a home.

The Elephants

Four lovely elephants
painted on the wall
four regal elephants
stately and tall

Four lovely elephants
total the sum
each lovely elephant
ran shy of the gun

Who'd shoot an elephant
tell me, who would
i'd find it hard to believe
anyone could

The Cup

a monologue

It's Melbourne Cup Day and the wind is blowing right off
the ice. Right off the ice.
I'm repeating what I'm saying because I don't think that
anyone can hear me. Their ears
are covered with woollen caps and there's not a soul about
not wearing long trousers.
The ladies' fashions have gone to the dogs. Only a fool would
go out in a summer suit.
However, it's Melbourne so anything could happen and by
early afternoon the sun will
come out and the dresses will be worn and the
photographers'll have their craft ready for
tomorrow's papers so it's been a waste of time talking about
the weather and how cold
it's been. It's Melbourne's best day of the year. Everything
closes down. Well, to a
degree. Even the most wowser of wowsers has a bet on the
cup. Well, to a degree there
I suppose. Once a wowser always a wowser I suppose you
could say. There's nothing
worse than a very heavy gambler and there's nothing worse
than a wowser. Gamblers come
in degrees perhaps but wowsers are wowsers. It's a
phenomenon I suppose but they tell me
it's true that to be a wowser you must inherit the gene. True or
false? It's anyone's guess just as it is anyone's guess which horse
will come first, be it an outsider or not. My money is on one
from New Zealand.

So up with your umbrellas or off with your raincoats and, as they say in Melbourne, as they
say almost everywhere else these times, tooth-achingly so,
'Have a nice day.'

Four Letters

And 'nice' is a four-letter word
And that's good
It is good that it's 'nice'
And it's nice that it's good

In this world that is changing
At rapid speed rate
A too-often four-letter word used
is 'hate'.

That's Joni Mitchell Singing in the Background

That's Joni Mitchell singing in the background.
A summer evening underneath the stars
A lonely soul looking for a friendship
Is this the year of Jupiter or Mars?

Joni Mitchell's magical performance
More stars aglow and shining
From above
How Joni Mitchell
Sings to such
Perfection

Perhaps some lonely soul
Will find someone to love.

Robots

You can't touch the soul of a robot
Tickle his chin for a laugh
Stand in a queue at the end of the day
Seeking his autograph.

You would be quite a fool if you thought so
See reason, just sit down and think
That a robot will do you out of a job
His eyelashes can't even wink.

Vote if you can against him
Push him right out of the queue
When you hear they are making a Robot
Protest, and I will come too.

People need work to make money
Some people are dying for food
The thought that robots are emerging
Puts me in a really bad mood.

Mechanical men need oiling
They will rust if they don't get their share
I'm appealing right now to the masses
Is anyone listening out there?

A human being needs water
A robot can't marry a banker's daughter
Or dance to a tune
Created by Porter

The idea of a robot is crazy; absurd
In fact I refuse to hear one single word
That praises them, favours them,
Wants to spend days with them.
I'd much rather a human
With all of his faults
Than a tin man constructed
With strings wires and bolts.

The Cup

Melbourne, Flemington.
It has to be THE CUP
Those racing fans
They still talk of Phar Lap

Those eyes of his
The form

He's in the Museum now.
A child says
THOSE TOM BOWLERS;
She speaks of his eyes
They remind her of alleys
And those around her laugh

Remembering

Do you remember when we all read Maugham?
Saw films and plays that shone with great success?
Some books we looked upon as treasures
Reread them and never loved them less.
I Think my favourite story was 'The Letter'
Bette Davis brought the role onto the screen
It was many years ago I saw the movie
I remember thinking then
it was the greatest film
that I had everseen.

Plumb Roles

Hamlet and Cleopatra
What plumb roles
He for Hamlet she for Cleo
Together what a
Magic duo
Scripts of course would
Differ greatly
But of the actors
I've seen lately
Male and female could
Equally perform as good.

Diving

I'm off to do some diving
Down in the ocean deep
All that salty water
Could waken me from sleep

I've been driving on the freeway
And it hasn't been much fun
But the ocean is large and it's also cold
And already I'm missing the sun.

Onions

I'm peeling onions
And the tears run down my face
I'm at the kitchen sink
Stand back apace
It's a comical situation
You probably agree
An inexpensive exercise
As all these tears run free!

Tell Me Something That I Do Not Know

There's a war going on.
Tell me something that
I do not know.
Tell me there is no war
Going on
That may amaze me
That will be something
That I really don't know

That will be something that
I wish to know
Something that I never
Thought that I would ever know.

Rivers

If all the rivers in the world dried up
And we had to drink sea water
We'd be sorry as sin
And terribly thin
And our time on this Earth
Would be shorter.

Hamburger With the Lot

You have to laugh
It's on the order board
'HAMBURGER WITH THE LOT'.

My friend Chloe,
You have to laugh,
She orders her 'HAMBURGER WITH THE LOT'
Without the onion, the beetroot,
The cheese, the sauce.

I try to understand her plan
and see some value
But without the sauce?
No hamburger is a hamburger
Without the sauce
No matter which way you look at it.
Well, not in my scheme of things.
You have to laugh.

The Birds

They rise earlier than we do
Daylight saving means not a thing
All birds love to sing
They do not seem to age as we do

No morning sleep in for them
Nor late-night partying
No irritability
(unless you are a miner or a
Nesting magpie
Or, come to think of it,
A butcher bird).
What a contradiction you are.

Your morning call
Defies description
Sends messages of
Joy and welcome.
Who writes your song?

You are forgiven for
Waking me early.

Raindrops

The smell of the raindrops
Is like manna from the Gods
Precision-like they fall
Upon the street of your dreams.

The Palace

They called it the coffee palace
Those sisters who owned it
It was a first you could say
In those days of the past

A sort of refined version
Of a pub as I remember it
But the coffee was different
You noticed the aroma streets away

And you drank it strong
Or made on milk
Unless you ordered it
Straight black
Piled the sugar in
And drank it hot

So many blends and changes
In today's market
And advertising plays its part
Along with the controversy
'It's good for you, It's not'
'It's not good for you, it is'
And don't forget the
Barista who serves it with a smile.

Statistics

I love numbers
Except perhaps of course
For just a few
Superstition always plays its part
In numbers
Some people will never entertain
The number two
I don't want to know the reason
For that theory
Thirteen is the number I deplore
Everyone of course will have
Their favourite
I have never heard a soul
Talk ill of 'four'
It's unlucky to be superstitious
My father always said
And that amused us
He said it with a twinkle in his eye
His message was a strange one
And ironic
The number that our dad said
That he hated most
Was the number of the day
He was to die.

Always in a Hurry

Always in a hurry
What happened to
'slow down you go too fast?'
Isn't the journey better
than the destination
Or wasn't it?
And how the journey's changed
The freeways have seen to that
Those concrete jungles
Where once gum tree smells
And cool fresh breezes blew
For something new
The journey's a nightmare
You wonder at the
Worthwhileness of it.

The Boa Constrictor

I wonder what Noah
Thought of the boa
One day perhaps
We will learn

He's a very big snake
And make no mistake
He's much larger by far
Than the worm.

Upon Retirement

Let us cook a chook
Sit out in the sun
Beside the babbling brook
And read a book

Let's think about
The time it took
To cook the chook
And read the book

And not forget
James Captain Cook
Who sailed out here
To take a look.

That Moon

If man landed on the moon
As most believed he did
I could bet a golden dollar
You could bet a million quid
That someone some day
Will prove us right
And others prove us wrong
And make another million
And write a famous song.

Blue Wrens

One thing better than
One blue wren
Is two.

How ordinary
Is the swallow
But his mum loves him
As good mums do.

And she would also
Given choice
Bank on two.

Fantasy

Into the world of fantasy
I place my trust
With no other place to go to
I go there if I must

The world goes on without me
If so I chose to roam
And given time for second thoughts
Most likely I'll come home.

Lizz Murphy Asks a Question

Lizz Murphy asks a question:
Do fish ever get seasick?
I think Lizz Murphy's question
Deserves a giant tick

It's a funny sort of question
Not one that all would ponder
But it set my mind a thinking
As I took myself to wander

I wondered over hill and dale
Thought about the largest whale
Saw him swimming in the ocean
Wondered if he had a notion

Dismissed the question in the end
Talked about it with a friend
Enjoyed the laughter for a while
Good to see a happy smile

The question Lizz is sort of odd
And funny and obtuse
But I am not to answer it
That's it. There's no excuse!
I doubt that we will ever know
The answer to the quote
But it was very funny Lizz.
We laughed at what you wrote!

Once

Once, when law-abiding citizens
Were the norm
Locksmiths made their money
Taking care of banks and other
Big time establishments
But business is booming
There's a fortune to be made
Everybody needs a locksmith.

I had a kilo of butter taken from
My esky whilst on a camping trip
Up north. The butter wasn't even
Frozen. I question if I need one to
Key in butter, it's enough to make
your thoughts melt.

If They Fluoridate the Water

From the tap above my
kitchen sink
I cannot offer you a drink
The fluoride from the water tap
Could claim you in a single zap
Pure water from a pristine stream
Is non-existent
Just a dream
Those are the words
That will be said
Long after we are
Gone and dead.
Once other countries had a go
Then after usage all said NO.

Just How the Blackbird Sings

The constant dripping of the kitchen tap
The buzzing of the bee
      I think of the annoyance
That these sounds can make to me.

My eyes land on the deaf man
Who doesn't know these things
But then, alas, this deaf man
Knows not how sweet the blackbird sings.

www.ingramcontent.com/pod-product-compliance
Lightning Source LLC
Chambersburg PA
CBHW062207100526
44589CB00014B/1995